ALL ABOUT Light

LEON GRAY

raintree

a Capstone company — publishers for children

Raintree is an imprint of Capstone Global Library Limited, a company incorporated in England and Wales having its registered office at 264 Banbury Road, Oxford, OX2 7DY – Registered company number: 6695582

www.raintree.co.uk
myorders@raintree.co.uk

Original illustrations © Capstone Global Library Limited 2020
Originated by Capstone Global Library Ltd
Printed and bound in India

ISBN 978 1 4747 7721 6 (hardback)
ISBN 978 1 4747 7727 8 (paperback)

British Library Cataloguing in Publication Data
A full catalogue record for this book is available from the British Library.

Acknowledgements
We would like to thank the following for permission to reproduce photographs:
Cover: Shutterstock: Janaka Dharmasena. Inside: Dreamstime: Ajn 3, 37, Americanspirit 43, Andyb1126 12, Barsik 15, Bdingman 42, Bear66 23b, Cammeraydave 9, Clarsen55 29b, Costa007 20, Dead Morozzzka 13, Duskbabe 28, Dzain 22, Fireflyphoto 10, 11, Glazyuk 41, Ig0rzh 6, Igordabari 7, Iofoto 5, Miloszbudzynski 24, Nikkytok 38, Niserin 39, Parrus 30, Petarneychev 4, Ruslasker 25, Sonyae 27, Stevemcsweeny 32, Sugar0607 23c, Trilobite 29t, Verastuchelova 18, Y0jik 26; NASA: NASA/JPL-Caltech/UCLA 21; Shutterstock: Ozerov Alexander 16b, Andresr 19, Darren Baker 40, Maxim Blinkov 2, 45, Ensuper 14, Warren Goldswain 8, Fer Gregory 16t, Kostudio 35, Leonidtit 44-45, Maxart 31, MilanB 17, Michal Ninger 33, Edyta Pawlowska 34, Konstantin Sutyagin 36.

Every effort has been made to contact copyright holders of material reproduced in this book. Any omissions will be rectified in subsequent printings if notice is given to the publisher.

All the internet addresses (URLs) given in this book were valid at the time of going to press. However, due to the dynamic nature of the internet, some addresses may have changed, or sites may have changed or ceased to exist since publication. While the author and publisher regret any inconvenience this may cause readers, no responsibility for any such changes can be accepted by either the author or the publisher.

Contents

What is light?

Every time the Sun rises in the sky, our world is filled with natural sunlight. In fact, light is all around us – even at night, when we flick a switch to light up a dark room.

Light around us

Natural light comes from the Sun – a ball of gases that spews heat and light into space. The Sun is so hot that it can light up our planet from millions of kilometres away. The Sun lights up only half of the planet during the daytime. At night, that half of the planet is covered in darkness.

Lighting up the dark

People have found ways of lighting up their lives without the Sun. Today, electricity is our main source of man-made light. Whenever you flick a light switch you are using electricity to light up the darkness.

The Sun is a star, which burns very brightly and provides our planet with both light and heat.

LIFE WITHOUT LIGHT

Imagine a world without light. It would be cold and dark. There would be no colour. Our planet would not be a very nice place to live. In fact, you would not be able to survive because nothing on Earth can live without light.

Waves and light

Scientists think that light sometimes acts like waves that pass through the air like ripples on a pond. At other times, light acts like particles that shoot through the air at an incredible speed.

Helpful light

Light is important in many ways. It provides plants with energy to make food. In turn, the plants are food for animals, including people. Today, scientists are trying to find ways to use the energy from light to make electricity.

No life on Earth would be possible without the Sun.

Chapter One
Lighting up our lives

Light is everywhere – most of it is from the Sun, but it also comes from fires, candles, torches and neon lights. Light also shines from electronic gadgets such as computer monitors, smartphones and television screens. There are also some animals that give out light.

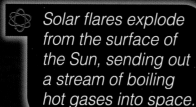
Solar flares explode from the surface of the Sun, sending out a stream of boiling hot gases into space.

What is the Sun?

The Sun is our closest star. Stars are giant balls of hydrogen and helium. Most of the hydrogen is found at the centre (core) of the Sun. It is so hot there that the hydrogen changes into helium. As this happens, the Sun releases huge amounts of heat and light.

The universe contains billions of galaxies, each containing millions or billions of stars – just like our own Sun.

Day and night

The Sun shines all the time, but we see sunlight only during the day. At night, the sky turns to darkness. This happens because the planets in the solar system spin around the Sun in a path called an orbit. Earth also spins on its own axis as it orbits the Sun. It takes 24 hours for Earth to make a complete turn. At any time, half of the planet faces towards the Sun, and it is daytime. The other half faces away from the Sun, and it is night-time.

LIFE WITHOUT THE SUN

What would happen if the Sun suddenly stopped shining? The first thing you would notice is the darkness. In a few hours, you would be very cold. Gradually, the water in ponds and rivers would freeze. Plants and animals, including people, would very quickly starve and die.

7

Turn on the lights

In prehistoric times, people started fires to light up dark nights. Over time, they used the light from fires in candles and oil lamps. Then, in the late 1800s, people began to use electricity to create light.

Light sources

Something that gives out light is called a light source. The Sun is a natural source of light, but we also use other things to light up our lives. In prehistoric times, people used twigs and branches as fuel for their fires. Later people invented other ways to light up dark nights. For example, candles burning wax and lamps fuelled by gas and oil.

The electric age

In the late 1800s, scientists began experimenting with electricity as a way of making light. American inventor Thomas Edison and English scientist Joseph Swan made the first practical light bulbs. Even today, light bulbs are still based on these early designs.

A DJ uses laser light to mix and play music on a CD player.

Light bulbs

A light bulb is a gas-filled glass bulb.
It contains a thin wire (filament) made from a metal called tungsten. When you flick a light switch, electricity flows through the tungsten. The filament heats up to 2,480 °C (4,500 °F) and glows white hot.

Bright lights

Some modern light bulbs are made without tungsten filaments. For example, neon lights consist of a glass tube filled with neon gas. When electricity flows through the gas, the neon atoms produce energy to make the bulb glow.

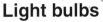

The tungsten filament of a light bulb glows brightly when electricity flows through it.

SUPER SCIENCE FACT

An energy-saving light bulb uses a lot less electricity than a traditional incandescent bulb. It also lasts much longer.

Other light sources

Most light sources, such as candles and the Sun, give off heat as well as light. Some materials give off light without creating any heat, while some animals make their own light – just like living light bulbs!

Heat and light

When light sources give off heat as well as light, it is called incandescence. When a material produces light without creating heat, it is called luminescence.

Glow in the dark

The hands of some wristwatches glow by luminescence so that you can tell the time in the dark. The hands of the watch are coated with a substance that absorbs light during the day and then gives off light at night. The signs above emergency exits are another example of luminescence. These signs are made from luminous paint, which glows in the dark so that people can find their way.

The glow-in-the-dark material that coats the hands of this watch gives off light by luminescence.

Living light

Some animals produce light in a process called bioluminescence. Their bodies glow to send signals to each other or lure prey towards them. The firefly mixes chemicals inside its body, and the reaction creates a flash of light. The firefly flashes to "talk" to other fireflies.

The light that is emitted by the bodies of animals such as fireflies is called bioluminescence.

SUPER SCIENCE FACT

Can you imagine living in total darkness all the time? Some animals, such as deep-sea anglerfish, live in the darkest depths of the ocean and never see the light of day. The anglerfish has light that glows from a stalk on top of its head. It uses the light as a lure to attract prey.

Chapter Two

Nature of light

It took scientists hundreds of years to work out what light is. Light is a form of energy called electromagnetic radiation. Light travels in waves, like all forms of electromagnetic radiation. It is made up of tiny particles called photons.

SUPER SCIENCE FACT

People rely on invisible forms of light all the time. Doctors use X-rays to take pictures of broken bones. Aeroplane pilots use radio waves to help them stay on course. People use microwave ovens to cook food. You use infrared light whenever you change channels on the TV using a remote control.

Scientists use radio telescopes to collect and study the radio waves given off by objects such as stars.

Energy changes

There are many different forms of energy and energy can change from one form into another. For example, a torch needs batteries to work and batteries store chemical energy. When you turn on the torch, the chemical energy changes into electrical energy. The electrical energy then flows through the filament in the light bulb, changing into heat energy and light energy. The bulb then glows, giving out light so that you can see in the dark.

Electromagnetic spectrum

The light we see is only a tiny fraction of all the light in the universe. There are other forms of invisible light: ultraviolet light, infrared light, X-rays, gamma rays, microwaves and radio waves. All the different forms of visible and invisible light make up the electromagnetic spectrum.

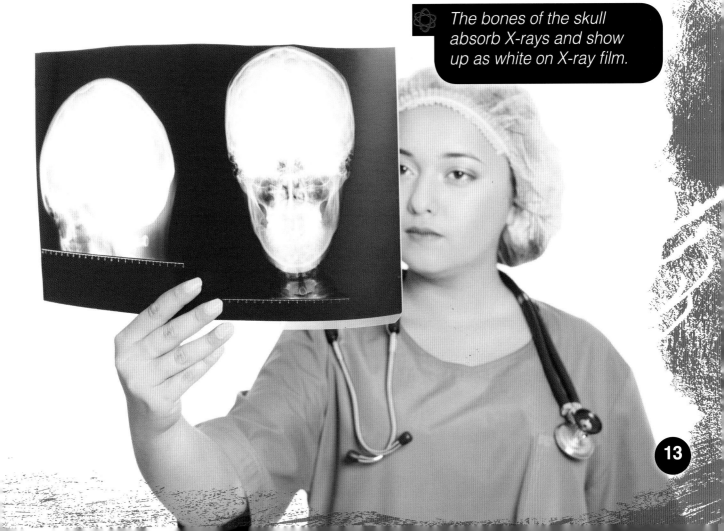

The bones of the skull absorb X-rays and show up as white on X-ray film.

13

Light waves

To heat and light up our planet, light must travel from the Sun to Earth. How this happens has puzzled scientists for hundreds of years.

Light waves

About 400 years ago, Italian scientist Francesco Grimaldi studied the shadows made by candles. He found that the shadows were wider than they should be and suggested that the light from the candles had bent like a wave.

Light waves travel a bit like the ripples of water on the surface of a pond.

Young's experiment

It took another 200 years to prove that light travelled in waves. The English scientist Thomas Young shone light through a narrow slit in a piece of cardboard. The light formed a ripple of waves, like the waves that travel across the surface of a pond when you throw a pebble in the water. Young also worked out the length of the waves. He showed that each wave measured less than one millionth of a metre.

LIFE WITHOUT YOUNG'S EXPERIMENTS

Much of our modern-day understanding of physical science stems from the results of Young's experiments. For instance, Young showed how the lens in an eye changes shape to focus on objects (see pages 34–35).

Wave shape

Light waves have a curved shape, similar to waves on the surface of an ocean. There are high points and low points that occur again and again. Light waves have three main features:

wavelength: the distance from one point on a wave to the same point on the next wave, usually measured from high point to high point

amplitude: the height of the wave from its high point to its mid-point

frequency: the number of waves that pass by every second.

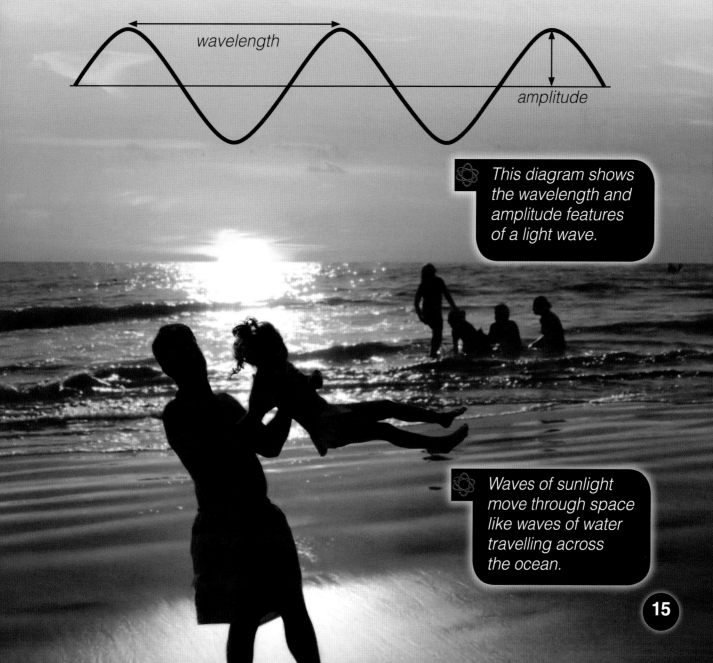

wavelength

amplitude

This diagram shows the wavelength and amplitude features of a light wave.

Waves of sunlight move through space like waves of water travelling across the ocean.

Colours of light

Sunlight consists of many different colours. Usually, we cannot see the separate colours because they combine to make natural white light. But sometimes you can see the colours of white light – for example, when sunlight passes through raindrops and a rainbow appears in the sky.

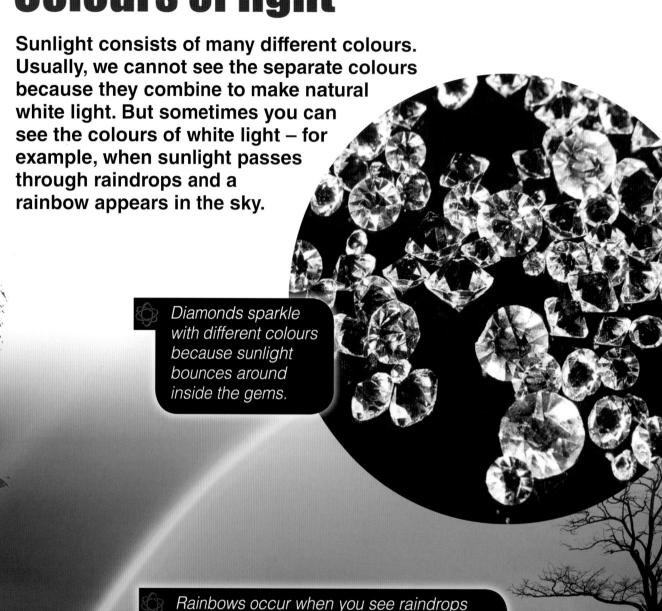

Diamonds sparkle with different colours because sunlight bounces around inside the gems.

Rainbows occur when you see raindrops fall in front of sunlight. Each raindrop separates the sunlight into colours.

Spectrum of light

The pattern of colours found in white light is called a spectrum. There are seven main bands of colour in the spectrum. They are red, orange, yellow, green, blue, indigo and violet. These bands of colour blend into each other so that our eyes can see millions of different colours.

Wavelengths

Different colours exist because light waves are different lengths. The longest waves appear as red light. The shortest waves appear as violet light. In between, there are different wavelengths for orange, yellow, green, blue and indigo.

Newton's experiment

In 1665, British scientist Isaac Newton discovered the different colours of white light during an experiment in a dark room. He put a triangular wedge of glass, called a prism, on a table and opened the curtains to let a ray of light shine through. The prism split the sunlight into the spectrum of colours. Newton used a second prism to focus the spectrum back into white light, which shone onto the wall behind the scientist.

A prism splits white light into a spectrum of colours.

LIFE WITHOUT COLOUR

Imagine a world without any colour. All you would see would be shades of black, white and grey. It would be like living in an old black-and-white film.

Particles of light

Scientists were puzzled when they found out that light travels in waves. They knew that waves need something in which to travel – for example, ocean waves travel as ripples in the water and sound waves travel as ripples through the air. Scientists wondered how light could travel in waves through the emptiness of space.

Balls of light

Isaac Newton was the first person to come up with an answer. He thought that light consisted of tiny particles. Looking at his reflection in a mirror, Newton suggested that light particles bounced off the surface of the mirror just as balls bounce off a wall. Newton's idea of particles explained why light could travel through empty space.

Particles of light bounce off the surface of a mirror to create a reflection of this girl's face.

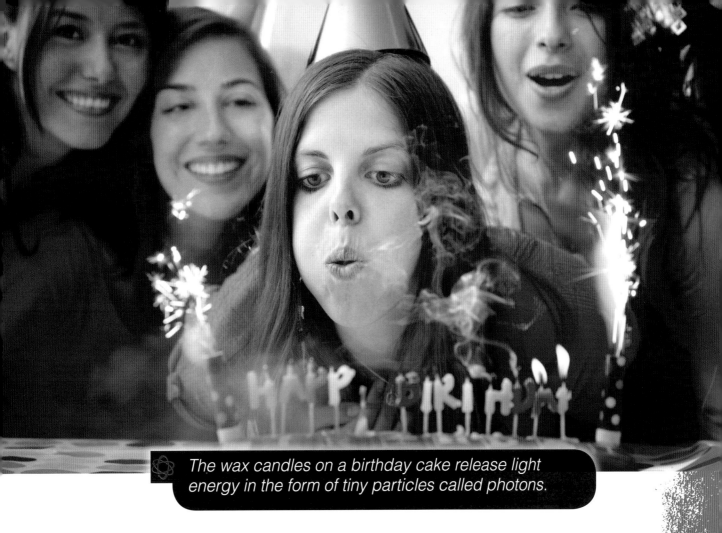

The wax candles on a birthday cake release light energy in the form of tiny particles called photons.

Unlocking the atom

Newton's idea was well ahead of his time. For hundreds of years, no one could prove that these light particles even existed. At the beginning of the 1900s, scientists unlocked the secrets of the atom. In 1905, Albert Einstein showed that atoms sometimes release energy as tiny "packets", or particles, of light. These particles later became known as photons. Photons have no mass and travel out from the source of light, whether that is a candle, a torch or the enormous Sun itself.

SUPER SCIENCE FACT

Scientists now know that light can act as a wave and as a particle. Sometimes, light particles whizz through the air at an incredible speed. At other times, light moves through the air like ripples on the surface of a pond.

Chapter Three
Bouncing and bending

Sunlight travels through space in straight lines, and it moves incredibly quickly. If light hits a surface, it can also bounce off it and shoot off in a completely different direction. Light can also change direction when it passes through different materials.

Bright lights bounce around the stage at a music concert to create a spectacular visual display.

Light speed

The Sun is more than 149 million kilometres (92 million miles) away, but it takes the sunlight only eight minutes to reach our planet. Scientists have calculated that light travels at an incredible 299,792 kilometres (186,282 miles) per hour in the emptiness of space. Nothing in the universe can travel faster than the speed of light.

SUPER SCIENCE FACT

After the Sun, Earth's next nearest star, *Proxima Centauri*, is more than four light years away. So the next time you look at a star in the night sky, note that you are actually looking back in time!

Light years

Scientists use the speed of light to describe the huge distances between objects in space. They measure distances in light years. One light year is the distance light travels in one year, which is 9.5 trillion kilometres (5.9 trillion miles).

Slowing down

Light travels so quickly in space because there are no atoms or molecules to get in its way. Light does not travel as quickly when it passes through objects such as air, glass or water. Light particles bump into the atoms and molecules in these materials and this slows down the light.

Light from the stars in the Andromeda galaxy takes 2.5 million years to reach Earth.

Light reflections

When light waves strike the surface of some objects, they bounce off and shoot away in a new direction. This is called reflection.

Light rebounds off the surface of a long reflection pool in front of the magnificent Taj Mahal in Agra, India.

Equal angles

When light reflects off a surface, the waves can either rebound straight back towards the light source or bounce off at an angle. The angle at which the light waves strike the surface is called the angle of incidence. The angle of reflection is the angle at which the light reflects away from the surface. The angle of incidence and angle of reflection are always the same. This is called the law of reflection.

Rough and smooth

When light waves strike a smooth surface, such as a mirror, the waves rebound in the same direction. Rough surfaces, such as rocks, scatter the light waves in all directions. This is because light hits the rough surfaces of the rocks at many different angles of incidence. This produces many different angles of reflection.

Uses of reflection

Reflection is important. We rely on reflections to see ourselves in a mirror. Huge reflecting telescopes allow people to look at faraway objects in great detail (see pages 40–41). Scientists also use the principle of reflection in optical fibres, which are used for communication (see pages 38–39).

The sides of a steep mountain valley appear as a reflection on the surface of a lake.

Light reflects off the smooth surface of these mirrored sunglasses.

LIFE WITHOUT REFLECTION

In a world without reflection, you would never see yourself in a mirror! In fact, you would not see anything at all. Every object would absorb light instead of reflecting it, so everything would appear black.

Bending the light

When light waves pass through certain substances, such as glass or water, the light slows down and seems to bend. This process is called refraction.

Passing through

Transparent (see-through) objects allow light waves to pass through them. When light travels through one transparent object, such as a glass, into another, such as water, the light waves slow down and change direction slightly. The light refracts, or bends.

Refraction makes the straw in this glass of water "bend" at the water's surface.

Changing speed

Refraction occurs because light travels at different speeds through different substances. Light travels more slowly in water than it does in the air. This is because water molecules are packed together far more closely than air molecules. The particles that make up light are more likely to hit water molecules than air molecules when light passes through the two substances.

Refraction in action

You can see refraction at work when you put a drinking straw into a glass of water. The part of the straw below the water level refracts light more than the part of the straw above the water. So the straw appears to bend at the surface of the water.

SUPER SCIENCE FACT

Have you ever seen a mirage on a road on a hot day? The mirage appears as a pool of water but it vanishes before you reach it. Mirages occur because sunlight bends as it moves between the layers of cool and warm air near the road's surface. The refracted light looks like ripples on the surface of a pond.

Refraction can play tricks on your eyes, for example, when a mirage appears on the surface of a desert.

Diffraction and scattering

Diffraction occurs when light passes through tiny gaps in objects and the waves spread out in all directions. Scattering occurs when light hits tiny particles in objects and then zooms away in all directions.

Diffraction

Thomas Young used diffraction to prove that light consists of waves. He showed that light waves passing through a narrow slit spread out like ripples of water on the surface of a pond. He also showed that light waves from different sources combine to create bigger waves or cancel each other out.

Colour in bubbles

You can see the effects of diffraction by looking at a soap bubble. Some light waves bounce off the outer surface of the bubble, while others bounce off its inner surface. On some parts of the bubble, the two reflections combine to produce bright colours. On others, the reflections cancel each other out and the bubble appears to be black.

Diffraction causes different colours to appear on the surface of a bubble.

Scattering

To see the effects of light scattering, look up at a blue sky. Before it reaches our eyes, sunlight passes through Earth's atmosphere. Some wavelengths of this light pass straight through the air. Others, particularly blue light, crash into air molecules and scatter. When you look up at the sky, you see the scattered light as a blue glow in the atmosphere.

SUPER SCIENCE FACT

The brilliant colours of auroras are the result of the scattering of sunlight. The Sun is constantly spitting out particles that become trapped in the magnetic field near Earth's polar regions. When these particles collide with air molecules, energy is released in the form of brightly coloured light.

On a clear sunny day, the sky appears bright blue. This is because air molecules scatter blue light from the Sun more than any other colour.

Chapter Four

Seeing the light

Our eyes are complex organs that take in light waves and change them into nerve signals. These signals then travel to the brain, which changes them into an image we can see.

Opening up

Our eyes see by letting in the light that bounces off different objects. Light waves pass through a hole, called the pupil, at the front of the eye. A ring of muscle, called the iris, changes the size of the pupil to control the amount of light that enters your eye. The iris shrinks in bright light to restrict the amount of light that enters each eye. When it is dark, the iris relaxes to let in more light.

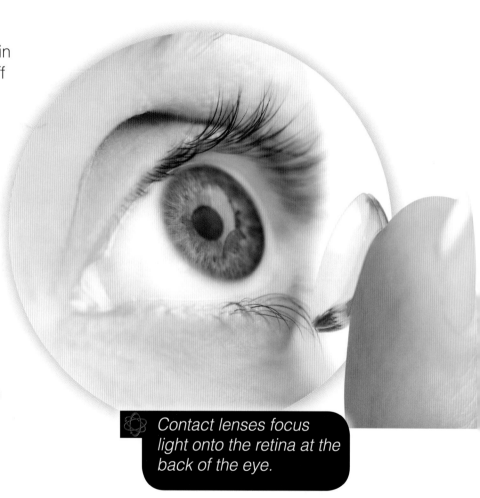

Contact lenses focus light onto the retina at the back of the eye.

Into focus

The lens in each eye focuses light rays onto the back of the eyeball, called the retina. Cells in the retina convert the light into electrical signals, which pass through the optic nerve into the brain. The brain processes these signals and forms the image you can see.

Some patterns can play tricks on our eyes. They are called optical illusions.

Rods and cones

The retina consists of cells called rods and cones. Rod cells pick out different shades of grey, while the cone cells are sensitive to different colours.

Seeing in colour

Our eyes see the light waves that bounce off objects. Different objects have different colours because they absorb and reflect different wavelengths of light.

Coloured sweets absorb and reflect different wavelengths of light. We see some objects as red because they reflect red light more than any other colour.

In colour

When light waves hit an object, only some of the light is reflected. For example, a red car reflects all the red wavelengths of white light but absorbs the blue, green and yellow wavelengths, so all you see is the red reflection. White objects reflect all the wavelengths, while black objects absorb all the light waves that hit them.

Our eyes split white light so we can see colourful images.

Newton's story

Isaac Newton discovered that visible light consists of a spectrum of colours that combines to make white light (see pages 16–17). He suggested that our eyes work like glass prisms, splitting white light into the different colours we can see. To test this, he stuck a knitting needle into the back of his eye and squeezed his eyeball to see if different colours appeared. The colours did not appear, Newton's eye became infected, and he nearly ended up going blind!

SUPER SCIENCE FACT

The cone cells on the retina are the eye's colour-detection system. Cone cells can detect only three different colours: red, green and blue. The brain combines these three main colour signals into all the different colours that we can see.

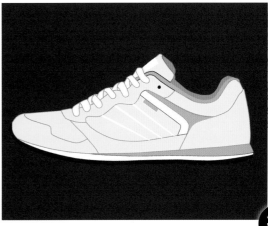

31

Animal eyes

Many animals rely on vision to make sense of the world. Some have simple eyes that can detect only light or dark. Others have highly developed eyes that are even more sensitive than our own.

Simple eyes

The "eyes" of animals such as worms are tiny light-sensitive eyespots. These animals cannot see images of objects in the same way that we can. Instead, the eyespots tell the difference between light and dark, so the animal can move towards the light.

Compound eyes

Many insects, such as bees and flies, and some crustaceans, such as lobsters, have compound eyes. Rather than a single lens, their eyes are made up of lots of tiny lenses. The animal's brain puts the information from each lens together to form the bigger picture. Animals with compound eyes can see very quick movements – if you have ever tried to swat a fly, you will know how good the insect's eyesight is!

The compound eyes of a housefly consist of hundreds of tiny lenses.

Some predators, such as owls, rely on their sharp sense of vision to hunt other animals.

Super vision

Predators use their excellent eyesight to hunt other animals. Birds of prey have the best animal eyesight. They can spot the tiniest movement of a mouse while they fly more than 3 kilometres (2 miles) above the ground. They can see so clearly because their eyes are packed with many more rods and cones than our own eyes.

SUPER SCIENCE FACT

Cats and some other animals have excellent night vision. They have a light-sensitive film on the back of each eye that reflects light back onto the retina. This is why a cat's eyes glow at night when it is caught in a beam of light.

Sight problems

Many people take their sense of sight for granted. But our eyes are delicate organs, and many people have problems with their vision.

Sight issues

The most common eye problems are short-sightedness (myopia) and long-sightedness (hyperopia). Myopia is when people have difficulty focusing on distant objects. As the muscles that control the lens become weaker, the eyes focus the light to a point just short of the retina. This makes the images seem blurry. Hyperopia occurs when the muscles that control the lens make the lens much thicker than it should be, and the eyes cannot focus on objects properly.

Wearing glasses helps focus light onto the retina at the back of each eye so people can see more clearly.

Seeing the light

Both myopia and hyperopia can be resolved by wearing glasses. The lenses of the glasses refocus any light shining into the eyes onto the retina, so the images are clearer. Doctors can also correct myopia and hyperopia with laser surgery. This operation reshapes the lens so the eyes can focus properly.

Blind people sometimes have guide dogs or use canes to help them get around.

Blindness

Some people are born blind. This may be because the brain cannot process nerve signals from the eyes, or there might be problems with the nerves themselves. People can also become blind later on in life. One of the most common causes of blindness is a disease called diabetes. In this condition, the vessels supplying blood to the retina leak, and the eyes fill up with blood. Doctors can fix this problem with surgery.

Chapter Five

Using light

People need light to see, but we also rely on it for other things. We need the energy in sunlight for plants to grow and to make electricity. Many different devices, from microscopes to cameras, also use light in some way.

Chemical reaction

Plants need sunlight to live and grow. They make food from the energy in sunlight in a process called photosynthesis. It involves changing water and a gas called carbon dioxide into a sugary food called glucose. Plants take in carbon dioxide from the air, and they suck up water and other nutrients through their roots. The reaction needs the energy from sunlight to take place.

Inside plants

Plants trap the energy from sunlight inside their leaves. The leaves are full of a green substance called chlorophyll, which absorbs the energy from sunlight to use in photosynthesis. Most plants have green leaves because they need chlorophyll for the process of photosynthesis.

Plants use light to make food in a process called photosynthesis.

Towards the light

Plants need light for photosynthesis, so they will always grow to get as much light as possible. Seedlings grow up out of the soil towards the light. Scientists have even grown plants that can find their way through dark mazes to get to the sunlight.

The heads of these sunflowers always face towards the Sun to get as much light as possible.

LIFE WITHOUT PLANTS

What would happen if there were no plants in the world? Most animals eat plants, or they eat other animals that feed on plants. So without plants, every other living thing on the planet would die, including people!

Cameras and communication

Many different electronic gadgets make use of light. Cameras capture the light from objects in a similar way to the human eye, then store the images as a digital file. Another important use of light is in fibre optics, which use pulses of light to send messages between different locations.

Fibre optic cables stretch for hundreds of kilometres, carrying messages as tiny pulses of light.

The first camera

The earliest camera was the camera obscura. It was invented more than 1,000 years ago. The camera obscura consisted of a dark room with a hole in one side that let in sunlight. The light formed an upside-down picture on the other side of the room. Artists used the camera obscura to draw by tracing over the outline of the image.

Modern cameras

Most digital cameras work in the same way as your eyes. Light shines through a lens at the front of the camera. The camera stores the image as an electronic file.

Fibre optics

Fibre optic cables are glass or plastic tubes that carry messages in the form of pulses of light. The tubes are incredibly thin, but they can carry a lot of information such as computer files or the sound of your voice on the phone.

SUPER SCIENCE FACT

In the early 1800s, a French scientist called Joseph Niépce invented the first photographic film. He put light-sensitive chemicals on a sheet of metal and left the sheet inside a camera obscura. Over a period of time, the light formed a lasting image on the metal sheet.

A digital camera uses electronic sensors to capture the light reflected from an object and convert it into a computer file.

39

Microscopes and telescopes

Microscopes and telescopes are useful tools for doctors and scientists. Microscopes make tiny objects appear much bigger so we can see them. Telescopes bring faraway objects into focus so they can then be studied.

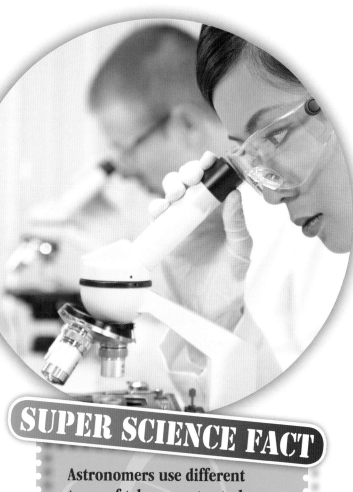

Compound microscopes can reveal objects up to 2,000 times their normal size. They have a high resolution, which means they produce a sharp, clear image of the object in view.

Microscopes

The first microscope was invented in the Netherlands in the late 1600s. It had a single lens and could enlarge objects by around 250 times. Modern microscopes have many lenses and can enlarge objects by 2,000 times or more. Doctors use microscopes to study the tiny cells found inside the human body.

SUPER SCIENCE FACT

Astronomers use different types of telescopes to study other forms of radiation, such as radio waves and ultraviolet rays, coming from distant objects. These telescopes detect these invisible forms of radiation and change them into images that we can see.

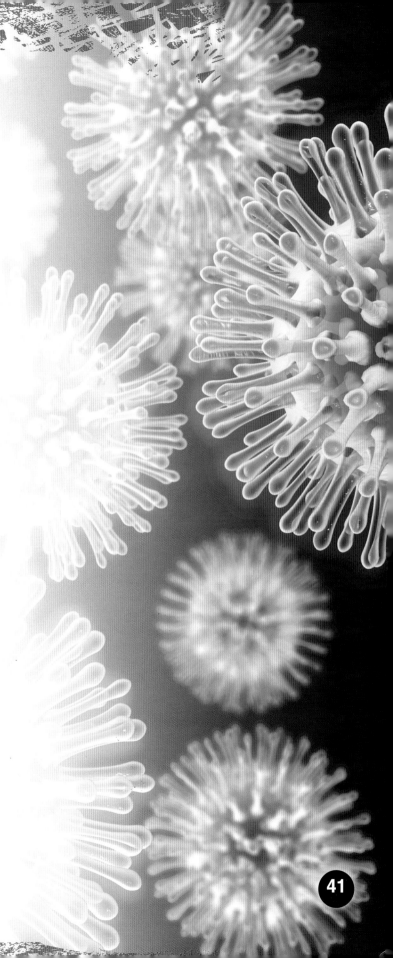

Different microscopes

Some microscopes do not use light to view objects. Electron microscopes fire beams of electrons at objects. The reflections of the electron beam build up to make a very detailed image of the object. The most powerful electron microscopes can reveal objects as small as an atom.

Telescopes

People use telescopes to look at faraway objects in the universe. Reflecting telescopes consist of a large, curved mirror at one end of a tube. The mirror reflects light from stars and other distant objects onto another flat mirror, which focuses the light into your eyes. Refracting telescopes use a curved lens to bend the light from distant objects onto another lens, which focuses the light.

An electron microscope reveals the complex structure of these virus particles. Electron microscopes use beams of electrons and electricity to provide a detailed picture of incredibly small objects.

Solar power

Most of the electricity we use comes from burning fossil fuels in power stations. Fossil fuels are running out, so we need to find new ways of making electricity.

Electricity from light

One way to create electricity is to collect the energy from sunlight and change it into electricity. This is called solar power.

Solar panels

The best way to collect energy from the Sun is via solar panels. These flat sheets are made from special photoelectric cells. The cells absorb most of the light that falls on them, which makes electricity flow through the panel. Wires then carry the electricity to a battery so it can be stored and used later.

A vast array of solar panels gathers the energy from sunlight and converts it into electricity.

Cells on the surface of this solar-powered racing car convert sunlight into electricity to power the electric motor.

Solar conversion

Some solar-power systems work in a different way. They consist of rows of mirrors that reflect the sunlight and focus it onto pipes filled with a special fluid. In countries with warm climates, the fluid can reach more than 400°C (750°F). This heat is then used to make steam, which turns a turbine to produce electricity.

Pros and cons

Solar power does not produce as much pollution as burning fossil fuels. And because the Sun shines every day, it can provide us with an unlimited supply of energy. But solar panels are expensive, and they can collect only a tiny amount of all the light energy that is emitted by the Sun.

A world of light

Light is all around us. Every day, the Sun shines down on our planet, lights up our world and lets us see our surroundings. This same light provides plants with the energy to make food. In turn, plants are food for people and other animals.

The Sun shines its warm light across the surface of our planet. Without it, we would not have the brightly coloured flowering plants that cover the slopes of this mountain.

Mysterious light

There are many different forms of light. Some of it we can see, but most is invisible. Scientists have studied light for centuries, and they are now beginning to understand how important it is. They are looking at the most distant light from faraway objects in space. They hope this will unravel the origins of the universe.

Making light

Thousands of years ago, the Sun was the only source of light. At night, the only thing that lit up the sky was other stars and sunlight reflected from the Moon. Eventually, people started fires to light up the night sky. They had found their own source of light.

Full circle

As people gained a better understanding of science, they came up with new ways of making light. First there were candles and torches. Then there were oil and gas lamps. Just 200 years ago, scientists used electricity to create light.

Today, the story has come full circle. Scientists are now using the energy in sunlight to create electricity.

SUPER SCIENCE FACT

Light is all around us, but we rarely notice it is there. Without light, we would not be able to see the world around us. We would live in total darkness – that's how blind people live their lives every day. Think about that the next time you flick on a light switch at home.

We now have spectacular laser light available to us.

Glossary

amplitude height of a wave from its high point to its mid-point

atoms tiny particles that make up everything in the universe

auroras shimmering bands of light in the night sky, common around the North and South Poles

bioluminescence light given off by living things

chlorophyll green pigment in plants that traps the energy from sunlight

diffraction when light waves spread out as they pass through a narrow gap

electricity flow of electrons through an object

electromagnetic radiation energy that flows through space as particles and waves

electromagnetic spectrum full range of energy waves that includes visible light, radio waves and X-rays

filament thin wire found inside many types of light bulb

fossil fuels fuels, such as coal, oil and gas, which have formed over millions of years from the remains of dead plants and animals

frequency number of waves that pass by every second

gamma rays form of electromagnetic radiation with a very short wavelength

helium colourless gas found in the Sun's core

hydrogen gas found throughout the universe, including in the Sun's core

incandescence when heat as well as light is given off by an object

infrared light form of electromagnetic radiation with a very long wavelength

lenses curved objects, such as the lens in your eyes, which are used to bend and focus light waves

light year distance light travels in one year

luminescence when light is created with the production of little, if any, heat

microwaves form of electromagnetic radiation with a very long wavelength

molecules combinations of two or more atoms

nerves fibres that pass electrical signals through the body

photons tiny "packets" or particles of light

photosynthesis process plants use to make food using the energy from sunlight

prisms triangular wedges of glass used to bend light

radio waves form of electromagnetic radiation with a very long wavelength

reflection when light bounces off a surface

refraction when light bends as it passes through an object

scattering when light bounces off an object and spreads out in all directions

solar power electricity made using the energy from sunlight

ultraviolet light form of electromagnetic radiation with a very short wavelength

wavelength distance from one point on a wave to the same point on the next wave

X-rays form of electromagnetic radiation with a very short wavelength

Find out more

Books

All About Physics (Big Questions), Richard Hammond (DK Children, 2015)

From Sunlight to Blockbuster Movies: An energy journey through the world of light (Energy Journeys), Andrew Solway (Raintree, 2016)

Light and Sound (Essential Physical Science), Louise and Richard Spilsbury (Raintree, 2014)

Sir Isaac Newton (Science Superstars), Angela Royston (Raintree, 2019)

Websites

www.bbc.com/bitesize/articles/zp7f8mn
Learn more about how the eye detects light.

www.dkfindout.com/uk/science/light
Find out more about light.

Index